IMAGES of America
FORT MORGAN

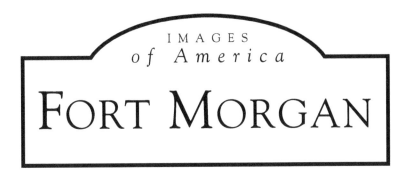

Bob England, Jack Friend,
Michael Bailey, and Blanton Blankenship

Copyright © 2000 by the Defenders of Fort Morgan
ISBN 978-1-5316-0369-4

Published by Arcadia Publishing
Charleston, South Carolina

Library of Congress Catalog Card Number: 00-102922

For all general information contact Arcadia Publishing at:
Telephone 843-853-2070
Fax 843-853-0044
E-mail sales@arcadiapublishing.com
For customer service and orders:
Toll-Free 1-888-313-2665

Visit us on the Internet at www.arcadiapublishing.com

Contents

Acknowledgments 7

Introduction to the Second Printing 8

1. Before Fort Morgan 9

2. Building the Fort at Mobile Point 13

3. The Civil War 21

4. The Era of Big Guns 45

5. World War II 113

Further Reading 124

About the Authors 126

Postscript 127

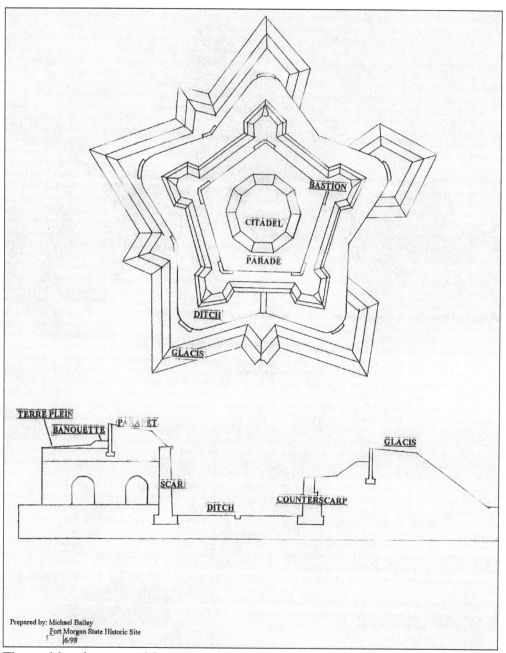

The citadel in the center of the original design of Fort Morgan provided shelter for the soldiers as well as a position for a last-ditch defense.

Acknowledgments

Those responsible for this book designed it to be an introductory photographic history of Fort Morgan. Many of the maps, drawings, and photographs published here are from the extensive collection of the fort's museum. Others, as marked, came from other collections. All of the illustrations testify to the rich history of Fort Morgan and its peninsula and how they fit into the larger fabric of America's past.

Fort Morgan came about because of collaborative efforts between the Defenders of Fort Morgan and the fort's staff, professionals who serve the state for the Alabama Historical Commission. Jim Parker, who coordinates archaeological and military properties, championed this work from the time of its conception. Jack Friend, Alabama Historical Commission member, wrote the introduction to the chapter on the Civil War. No one knows the story of the Battle of the Mobile Bay from his perspective. His passionate approach to the historical narrative has led him to sail Admiral Farragut's route several times. Michael Bailey, curator of the fort's museum, introduced the chapters on the Endicott period and the 20th-century service. Blanton Blankenship, site manager, contributed most of the captions to the illustrations and worked diligently to document the accuracy of the book.

At the Northwest-Shoals Community College, President Larry McCoy, Vice President Randy Parker, and Associate Dean Gary Wolfskill provided me with the time and resources needed to complete this project. Anita Kent, teaching assistant, contributed more help than she can know. Maxine Johnson, faculty secretary, typed this manuscript and manipulated the arcane details of computer work to submit the final project to the publisher.

Katie White, editor at Arcadia Publishing, possesses more patience than Job. She sent material at odd hours, talked us through many of the occult rituals of submission, and is as responsible for the final product as any of its contributors.

The Defenders of Fort Morgan, ably represented by C. Tom Hodges, Bob Neibling, and Dick Pugh, provided much of the stimulation and leadership for this work. But its real inspiration lies in another quarter. For 40 years, James Allen labored through the ranks of service to become chief of maintenance at Fort Morgan. His retirement left a gap that cannot be adequately bridged. Proceeds of the sale of this book contribute to a scholarship fund at Faulkner State Community College named in Mr. Allen's honor. It is to James Allen that this book is respectfully dedicated.

—Bob England
Northwest-Shoals Community College
Muscle Shoals, Alabama

Introduction to the Second Printing

The second printing of *Fort Morgan* calls for a celebration and maybe an explanation. The first printing sold quite well, but because of a number of events, the book's future looked bleak. The authors moved on to other projects. Jack Friend completed his magisterial study, *West Wind, Flood Tide: The Battle of Mobile Bay*. The United States Naval Institute Press published the book earlier this year. Jack's book promises to be the last word on Farragut's grand entry past the defenses of Fort Morgan. Blanton Blankenship and Michael Bailey continue their work at the historic fort. I assumed new duties at Northwest-Shoals Community College, taking on the additional responsibilities for the new Outdoor Leadership Program. I continue teaching as a member of the history faculty with a new research agenda.

The Defenders of Fort Morgan shifted focus slightly and, for several years, labored tirelessly on preservation and conservation issues that affect the entire Alabama Point area. Then Dick Pugh, past-president and a board member of the Defenders, initiated efforts that led to this second printing. Russell and Tammy Woerner, who own the Fort Morgan Marina, recognized the value of the book and persuaded Arcadia Publishing to crank up its presses once more.

To the community and its leaders near the fort go the credit for this printing of *Fort Morgan*. Any errors belong to the authors.

—Bob England
Northwest-Shoals Community College
February 2004

One

BEFORE FORT MORGAN

Fort Morgan guards the entrance to Mobile Bay. With Fort Gaines to the west on Dauphin Island, Fort Morgan stands as a reminder of the first comprehensive national defense plans to protect the United States. Though never tested in battle with a foreign power, Fort Morgan—and the other fortifications that watch over these shores—testifies to the 19th-century needs for unified policies to keep Americans safe and at peace.

Spanish explorers visited the lower Mobile Bay area but made no lasting impression. The French eventually settled the region. They built their first capitol at Twenty-Seven Mile Bluff but, sometime later, moved it first to Mobile and then to New Orleans. After the Seven Years' War—called the French and Indian War by Americans—Spain acquired all of Louisiana including New Orleans. But the area north of Lake Ponchartrain, in what is now Louisiana, as well as present-day southern Mississippi, lower Alabama, and Florida, became British territory. Mobile Bay became a part of West Florida. Pensacola was the colony's capitol. Other than Mobile, the major settlement was at Natchez. From 1765 until the outbreak of the American Revolution, British explorers, merchants, Native-American traders, settlers, and soldiers visited the region. But in 1779, the Kings of France and Spain—cousins—signed an alliance against England. Bernardo de Galvez, the intrepid governor of Louisiana, led Spanish and French forces along the Mississippi River and the Gulf Coast. Mobile fell to Galvez in 1780. In May 1781, Pensacola surrendered. The British presence in the Gulf of Mexico ended.

Despite Spanish success in the Wars of the American Revolution, Spain lost power internationally. Napoleon's invasion disrupted the country and Spain collapsed. Though Napoleon eventually lost his empire, the damage to Spain and to Spanish colonial interests could not be repaired. In the Spanish territories, pirates, outlaws, renegades, and desperadoes found a safe haven and an ideal location to threaten American settlements on the frontier.

At the same time, the United States and Great Britain moved closer to fighting over trading rights, maritime issues, and western difficulties with Native Americans. The U.S. possessed evidence that the British supported up-risings on the frontier from the Great Lakes to what is now south Alabama. In addition, Canadian lands beckoned to expansion-minded members of Congress who agitated for a war. These so-called "War Hawks" finally succeeded and in 1812 the United States Congress declared war on the British empire.

The U.S. Army promptly invaded Canada and failed. The British, on the other hand, landed their forces with near-impunity all over the Atlantic seaboard and Gulf Coast. The redcoats burned Washington, D.C., and threatened the mid-Atlantic states. A heroic defense at Fort McHenry in Baltimore Harbor ended British invasion attempts and His Majesty's Forces shifted their attention to the south.

Fresh from a successful campaign against the Creek Indians, Gen. Andrew Jackson assumed responsibility for the defense of the lower south and Gulf Coast. Gen. James Wilkinson, a Revolutionary War veteran, led an American column that captured Mobile and established control over the bay. Though Fort Conde guarded the old city, defenses had to be erected to protect the entrance of the bay. U.S. troops built Fort Bowyer on Mobile Point to thwart British invasion plans on the Gulf Coast.

—Bob England

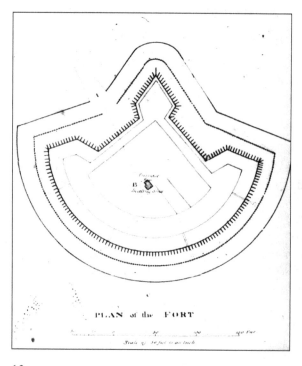

Fort Bowyer was a small fan-shaped work of sand and logs. The curved face covered the ship channel into Mobile Bay while one bastion and two demi-bastions provided land defense. Not only was the work too small for a proper defense against a siege, but it was also overlooked by sand dunes to the east. On September 14, 1814, a British naval attempt to shell the fort into submission was defeated with the loss of one ship. After their defeat at New Orleans in January 1815, the British launched a well-coordinated land and sea operation to reduce Fort Bowyer. Cut off and outnumbered, Lt. Col. Lawrence was forced to surrender his post on February 11, 1815. (National Archives and Records.)

The HMS *Hermes*, Captain W.H. Percy commanding, was the flagship of the four-ship British squadron that attacked Fort Bowyer on September 14, 1814. Anchoring within 100 yards of the fort, the *Hermes* exchanged gunfire with the small earthwork for more than three hours. The British attack failed and the *Hermes* was so badly damaged that she had to be abandoned. Set afire to prevent her from falling into enemy hands, the ship blew up at 10 p.m. (Fort Morgan Museum.)

William Lawrence served with distinction in the South during the War of 1812. He commanded Fort Bowyer during both of its engagements with the British. His victory over the British forces in September 1814 raised morale in the area and helped recruiting in the South. His actions won a commendation from Andrew Jackson and a brevet commission as lieutenant colonel. Following the Battle of New Orleans in January 1815, the British made a second attempt to capture Fort Bowyer. Avoiding mistakes, they soon established themselves in an earlier commanding position east of the fort. After a short siege Lawrence surrendered on February 11, 1815. Following the War of 1812, Lawrence continued to serve in the Army. He reached the rank of colonel in 1828 and resigned his commission in 1831. (Fort Morgan Museum.)

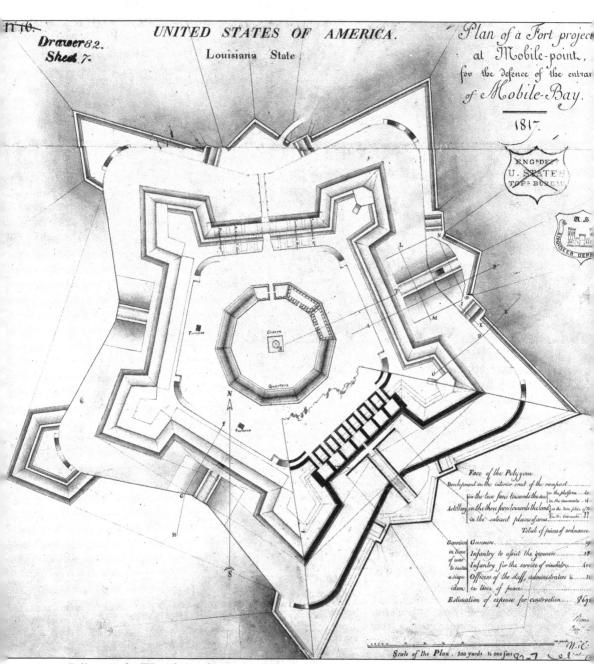

Following the War of 1812 the government determined to improve the nation's seacoast defenses. Simon Bernard, a former military engineer for Napoleon, was engaged to design plans for forts along the Atlantic and Gulf Coasts. His design for the works at Mobile Point—a pentagonal work with five bastions and a citadel—was a typical European design modified to the demands of the Gulf Coast. (National Archives and Records.)

Two

BUILDING THE FORT AT MOBILE POINT

Following the War of 1812 the United States embarked upon a major building program to improve the its seacoast defenses. On May 7, 1818, a contract was let with Benjamin Hopkins of Vermont to build a large masonry fort on Mobile Point at the entrance to Mobile Bay. He was to complete the work by July 1, 1821.

No one in Washington realized the enormity of Hopkins' task. Mobile Point was a frontier area. There were neither facilities available to make the large quantities of brick Hopkins would need, nor was lodging available for his laborers. Preparation costs far exceeded Hopkins' ability to pay and bankruptcy loomed. In August 1819, after working for a year, Hopkins died during a Yellow Fever epidemic. Captain R.E. DeRussey, the Corps of Engineers representative for the area, advised the War Department that Hopkins had accomplished almost nothing during his time on the Gulf Coast.

The federal government soon found another contractor willing to build the works at Mobile Point. Samuel Hawking of New York was awarded a contract on June 7, 1820. After arriving at Mobile Point he realized the task was far more than he could finance. He attempted to get out of his contract, but the government refused to make any concessions. In March 1821 Hawkins, heavily in debt, became ill and died.

With two contractors dead and still almost nothing accomplished at Mobile Point, the Army decided to let the Corps of Engineers direct the project. Rather than merely overseeing a contractor's progress, the Corps would be actively engaged in building the fort.

DeRussey assumed direction of the work as supervising engineer. He possessed wide authority to push the work through to completion. Using slave labor, which the other contractors had not done, he soon had the first walls of the fort under construction. However, the harsh climate took its toll on him also, and in July 1825 DeRussey transferred to New York for health reasons. His assistant, Lt. Cornelius Ogden, replaced him on Mobile Point.

Even with the project firmly in the hands of the engineers, the isolation and harsh conditions insured that the work progressed slowly. In 1833, as the project neared completion, the post was named Fort Morgan after Revolutionary War hero Daniel Morgan. Finally, in March 1834, almost 12 years after the original contract called for the project to be completed, Ogden turned the fort over to Captain F.S. Belton, Company B, 2nd U.S. Artillery.

—Blanton Blankenship

The French erected Fort Conde at Mobile, and at the conclusion of the French and Indian War the British, while occupying Mobile, changed the name of the to Fort Charlotte, after the wife of King George III. The Spanish took Fort Charlotte and Mobile in 1780. Until the building of fortifications on the lower bay, Fort Charlotte provided the only defense for Mobile. By the 1820s, the city expanded and the government demolished the old fort. This is a model of Fort Charlotte as it appeared in the 1770s.

Construction of the fort began in 1819. However, the inaccessibility of the site caused many delays and resulted in the bankruptcy of the first two contractors. The Corps of Engineers assumed responsibility for the completion of the fort in 1824 and saw the job through to its final completion in 1834. Although the fort took far longer to build and cost much more than was originally anticipated, the Army did not attempt to save time or money by significantly altering Bernard's plan. (National Archives and Records.)

These are the arched brick casemates of Fort Morgan. Each of the fort's five faces has seven casemates. The white deposits on the walls are lime that has leached out of the mortar through the years. Many of the casemates are unmodified from the time the fort was completed. (Fort Morgan Museum.)

This Lighthouse Service photograph, taken in 1859, shows the Mobile Point Lighthouse and the Lighthouse Gun Battery as they appeared on the eve of the Civil War. The living quarters for the lighthouse keeper are also visible. Penthouses were built over the cannon to protect them from blowing sand and salt air. (National Archives and Records.)

On March 7, 1834, Capt. F.S. Belton and Company B of the 2nd U.S. Artillery became the first soldiers to garrison Fort Morgan. They remained at the fort until October 1835, when they were transferred to Florida to aid in suppressing the Seminole Indians. During his stay on Mobile

Point, Belton painted several watercolor sketches of the fort. This one shows the fort and the large officers quarters building to the east. (Museum of the City of Mobile.)

This sketch shows the dry moat and Mobile Point Lighthouse. It also illustrates how close the ship channel was to the fort at that time. The small doorways in the bastions of the fort were deemed unnecessary and bricked up during a modernization of the post in the 1840s. (Museum of the City of Mobile.)

Three

THE CIVIL WAR

A little before midnight on January 3, 1861, Colonel John B. Todd and four companies of Alabama volunteers boarded the transport *Kate Dale* and steamed down the bay for Fort Morgan. They arrived at 3 a.m., and by sunrise the Alabama state flag had replaced the national flag. A Confederate soldier, writing from the fort that morning, said: "We found here about five thousand shot and shell; and we are ready to receive any distinguished strangers the Government may see fit to send on a visit to us." Eight days later, with Fort Morgan, Fort Gaines, and the Mount Vernon Arsenal occupied by state troops, Alabama seceded from the Union. A secession flag, which the women of Montgomery had made, "was raised over the Capitol, amidst the firing of cannons, the ringing of bells, and the shouts of the multitude." (1)

For the next three and one-half years, the Confederates worked to strengthen Mobile's lower defense line, which stretched 75 miles along the coast from the Florida border to Pascagoula, MS. During this period, the ram *Tennessee*, considered to be the most powerful warship afloat, was built and stationed in the lower bay. The *Tennessee*, Adm. Franklin Buchanan's flagship, and three gunboats, the *Morgan*, *Gaines*, and *Selma*, comprised the Confederate squadron; three forts—Morgan, Gaines, and Powell—were the key land fortifications.

The point of greatest concern to the Confederate high command and to Brig. Gen. Richard L. Page, commander of the lower defense line, was the Main Ship Channel opposite Fort Morgan—the only approach with enough depth to permit a serious attack by the Union navy. During the spring and summer of 1864, this passage was strewn with 180 mines and protected by 18 of the fort's heaviest guns. However, when the firepower of the Confederate naval squadron was added, a total of 34 guns could be brought to bear on an approaching enemy. Also, redoubts and trenches were constructed east of the fort to repel an attack by land.

This Parrot rifle fired a projectile that weighed 100 pounds. Cannon of this type were used from early in the Civil War until they were replaced by the advanced long-range disappearing rifles at the turn of the 20th century.

During the war, Fort Morgan provided covering fire for blockade runners entering and leaving the bay. At first one or two vessels comprised the blockade. Later, however, it was not unusual for a dozen ships to be stationed off the outer bar, with the smaller gunboats moving in closer at night. Although Mobile was considered a difficult port for blockade runners, the success rate was high. In 1864, before the Union gained control of the bay, 19 of 21 vessels that attempted to run-in were successful, and all of the 17 that ran out eluded capture. (2)

On August 5, 1864, the long awaited naval attack on Mobile's lower defense line commenced. At 6 a.m., 14 wooden vessels, lashed two abreast, and four ironclads steamed in from the Gulf. The lead ironclad, the *Tecumseh*, hit a mine and sank. Fearing a similar fate, the *Brooklyn*—the lead wooden vessel—stopped. This caused the next tow vessel—the *Hartford and Richmond*—to stop. With the Union attack stalled under the guns of Fort Morgan and the Confederate Squadron raking the line with deadly accuracy, the fate of the Union fleet hung by a thread.

Recognizing the peril, Adm. David G. Farragut, who was tied to the *Hartford's* port futtock shrouds high above the deck, ordered the fleet to cross the minefield. Following in the *Hartford's* wake, the other vessels crossed over without mishap (many of the torpedoes were duds), sank the *Gaines*, captured the *Selma*, and overpowered the *Tennessee*, but at a high price: a comparison of killed and wounded overwhelmingly favored the Confederacy—33 to 315. Control of the bay and the early surrender of

Fort Gaines now enabled Union ground troops to attack Fort Morgan, supported by naval gunfire. (3)

By August 9, Union troops, under the command of Maj. Gen. Gordon Granger, were transported across Mobile Bay to a landing site 4 miles east of Fort Morgan. By August 21, 25 cannons and 16 mortars were ready to fire. The next morning at daylight, a signal was given to commence the bombardment. From 7 a.m. to 9 p.m., the land forces and fleet fired with "unabated fury." At 9:30 p.m., however, a fire broke out in the fort, and the firing was "intensely renewed." At 6 a.m. the next morning, August 23, Brigadier General Page ordered a white flag to be raised and surrendered the garrison. (4)

Now under Union control, Fort Morgan would be used as a base for minor raids and as a staging area for the Battles of Spanish Fort and Blakely. In late August and early September, raids were staged on both sides of the lower bay; and in December, troops were landed at Pascagoula with orders to probe the western approaches to Mobile (these troops were repulsed at the Battle of Franklin Creek by Confederate cavalry). The raids, together with intelligence reports, convinced General Granger that a direct movement on Mobile from the west "would have encountered unequal resistance, and involved a protracted siege. It was therefore determined to flank them." (5)

On March 25, 1865, the XIII Corps, under the command of General Granger, moved by land around Bon Secour Bay to the small community of Marlow near Fish River. Here they were joined by the XVI Corps that had been transported across Mobile Bay from Fort Gaines. The two corps then marched north to participate in the Battles of Spanish Fort and Blakeley, both of which were fought after Lee's surrender at Appomattox.

—Jack Friend

1. Benson J. Lossing, *Pictorial History of the Civil War in the United States of America*, (Philadelphia Pa; George W. Childs, 1886), Vol. I, pp. 173–175.
2. Stephen R. Wise, *Lifeline of the Confederacy* (Columbia, S.C.; University of South Carolina Press, 1988), conversation with author.
3. Jack Friend, "Mobile Bay; First Strike for Grant's Strategy," *Mobile Register*, April 24, 1994, Section C, p. 1.
4. Christopher C. Andrews, *History of the Campaign of Mobile; Including the Cooperative Operations of General Wilson's Cavalry in Alabama* (New York; D. Ban Nostrand, 1876), pp 17–19.
5. Ibid, p. 31.

The Selma Independent Blues pose for a photograph before boarding a steamship to reinforce the Alabama State Troops garrisoning Fort Morgan early in 1861. Later in the war, the Blues formed part of the 8th Alabama Infantry Regiment. (Alabama Department of Archives and History.)

Julius Bayor, a member of the Grove Hill Guards, drew this pencil sketch of Fort Morgan in February 1861, shortly after Alabama militia occupied the post. He was killed on July 1, 1862, at Malvern Hill, VA, during Robert E. Lee's Seven Day campaign. (Alabama Department of Archives and History.)

The Confederates strengthened Fort Morgan's armament with heavier, more powerful cannons. The gun in the foreground is a 7-inch Brooke rifle, of Confederate design. Firing a 98-pound projectile over 4 miles, the Brooke was one of the best cannons of the war. The South's limited industrial capacity hampered the production. Only two of these heavy seacoast defense guns were provided for Fort Morgan. Sand traverses, added to give additional protection to the guns, hide the brickwork on the tip of the fort. (National Archives and Records.)

Fort Morgan was a subject of some interest in the North, as is shown by this engraving from *Harper's Weekly*. The first national Confederate flag flies over the fort, and the Mobile Point Lighthouse stands as a tempting target. (Fort Morgan Museum.)

Born in New York in 1828, Charles S. Stewart moved to Mobile, AL, when he was a young man. At the start of the Civil War, he cast his lot with the Confederacy. As captain of Company K, 21st Alabama Infantry Regiment, Stewart served with distinction at the Battle of Shiloh in April 1862. Promoted to lieutenant colonel, he commanded at Fort Morgan from October 1862 to April 1863. While observing the test firing of one of the post's cannon on April 30, 1863, he was killed instantly when the gun exploded and a 200-pound fragment of the piece struck him in the head. (Stewart Collection-Fort Morgan.)

This is the only known photograph of a member of the 1st Alabama Artillery Battalion in a Civil War uniform. Second Lt. Warren A. Anderson, Company B, served in the lower Mobile Bay defenses from 1862 until being captured in August 1864. Writing from Fort Morgan in January 1863, Anderson told his father ". . . I am very much in need of underclothing. My washerwoman has lost about half of what I brought here. There have been no new cases of small pox, and those who have it are getting well." (Fort Morgan Museum.)

Fort Morgan provided a refuge for ships bringing supplies to Mobile from Cuba. Union naval officers hesitated to risk their ships pursuing blockade runners directly under the fort's guns. (Fort Morgan Museum.)

J.H. Crownover, a member of Company C, 1st Alabama Artillery, drew this May Day card for his mother in 1863. Captured when Fort Morgan fell in August 1864, he was sent to a prisoner of war camp in Elmira, NY. While a prisoner of war, Crownover died of small pox on December 30, 1864. (Crownover Collection-Fort Morgan Museum.)

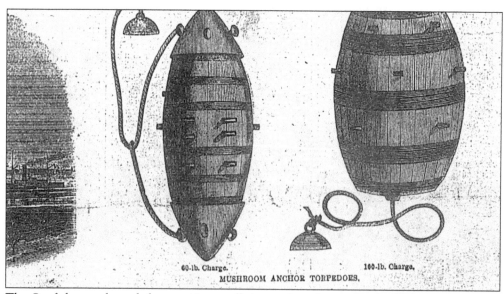

The Confederates depended upon mines, called torpedoes during the Civil War, to discourage any Union naval attempt to enter Mobile Bay. Two-thirds of the ship channel was mined, leaving only a narrow opening directly under the guns of Fort Morgan. To avoid the mines, Union warships had to pass the fort at point-blank range. (Fort Morgan Museum.)

This is one of two British-made 8-inch Blakely rifled guns. These guns ran the blockade at Charleston, SC, and went to Mobile by rail. Firing a 200-pound projectile, they were the most powerful guns in the fort at the time of the Battle of Mobile Bay. Unfortunately they had a slow rate of fire and proved of only limited value during the battle. The second Blakely was dismounted by Union fire. It is now on display at West Point Military Academy. (National Archives and Records.)

The Mobile Bay Squadron, commanded by Adm. Franklin Buchanan, was stationed at Mobile Point to assist Fort Morgan in defeating any Union navy attempt to enter the bay. The CSS *Tennessee*, an ironclad ram, was the flagship of the squadron. The three wooden warships, the *Selma*, *Morgan*, and *Gaines*, proved to be of only minimal value in action with the Union fleet. (Fort Morgan Museum.)

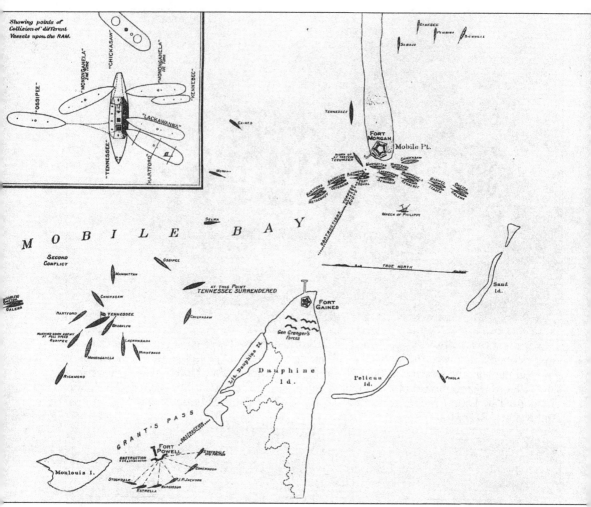

This original map illustrates the position of the Union and Confederate fleets during the Battle of Mobile Bay. The inset depicts the points on the *Tennessee* rammed by Union war ships. At the conclusion of the engagement, Farragut's victorious fleet anchored in the bay and Union soldiers laid siege to Forts Gaines and Morgan.

The CSS *Tennessee* was probably the best ironclad the Confederacy built. The 209-foot-long ship carried 6 inches of iron armor backed by 2 feet of wooden timbers. Her armament consisted of six Brooke rifled guns. She had two serious flaws—she was too slow and her rudder chains were exposed across her stern. During the Battle of Mobile Bay these two weaknesses proved to be fatal. (National Archives and Records.)

William Hughes commanded Company A, 1st Alabama Artillery Battalion, for most of the Civil War. During the Battle of Mobile Bay, his company manned the three guns of the Counterscarp Battery. One of his guns was dismounted and he was slightly wounded during the battle. While held prisoner of war in New Orleans, Hughes unsuccessfully tried to escape. (Fort Morgan Museum.)

At dawn on August 5, 1864, Adm. David G. Farragut boldly led his fleet of 14 wooden vessels and 4 ironclad monitors against Fort Morgan. Desperate efforts by the garrison of Fort Morgan failed to turn back the Union fleet. The Confederates fired 491 rounds at Farragut's ships but failed to sink any of them. As one disappointed soldier wrote, "We did all that it was possible for men to do."

The USS *Tecumseh*, leading the monitors into battle, crossed in front of the fleet's column of wooden ships in an attempt to attack the *Tennessee*. This unexpected move not only threw the Union column into disorder, but also carried the *Tecumseh* into the torpedo field. A tremendous explosion rocked the monitor and she sank within a minute. The monitor and 93 men of the crew, including the captain, fell victim to a Confederate torpedo.

Although his plans were disrupted by the sudden destruction of the *Tecumseh*, Farragut remained calm. With his way blocked by the sunken monitor and other stalled ships, he ordered his flagship to steam through the torpedo field. His bold gamble worked, as none of the other torpedoes exploded. The remainder of the fleet followed the flagship through the torpedo field, away from the guns of Fort Morgan and into Mobile Bay. (National Archives and Records.)

After fighting it way past Fort Morgan, the USS *Lackawanna* rammed the CSS *Tennessee*. The attack caused more damage to the *Lackawanna* than to the ironclad. (Fort Morgan Museum.)

Pictured is the surrender of the *Tennessee*.

On August 9, 1864, after the fall of Fort Gaines on Dauphin Island, Union troops landed 3 miles east of Fort Morgan and began siege operations. Shielded by sand dunes and protected by sharpshooters, Union artillery moved close to the fort in preparation for an overwhelming bombardment. An artist's rendition of the Union siege lines east of Fort Morgan shows a mortar position in the foreground. The mortars' high arching fire dropping shells inside the fort caused serious problems for the garrison. (Fort Morgan Museum.)

On August 22, 1864, the Union army opened a final crushing bombardment on Fort Morgan with 42 guns and mortars. The ships of Admiral Farragut's fleet joined in the action. The wooden ships fired their rifled guns at the fort from long range while the monitors closed to within less than 1,000 yards of the fort. (Fort Morgan Museum.)

The fort was battered during the siege, not only by army siege guns, but also by the Union fleet. This photograph of the western face of the fort shows damage done by the Union Navy. Two shells from monitors breached the bastion in the background—one hole is near the top of the wall, the other at the top of the right-hand embrasure. These two shots were the only ones during the siege to break completely through the fort's walls. (Fort Morgan Museum.)

A 30-pounder Parrott rifle is on exhibit in the Parade Ground at Fort Morgan. Eight of these guns, manned by the 1st Indiana Heavy Artillery, were used against the fort in August 1864. The heavy guns were manhandled over more than a mile of sand to reach their positions to fire at the Confederates. (Bob England Photo.)

Damage caused by Union siege guns is clearly visible on the left face of Bastion No. 1. This photograph, taken September 1864, shows that repair efforts by the U.S. Corps of Engineers are already underway. Visible in the dry moat are eight of the mortars that were instrumental in forcing the surrender of the fort. (National Archives and Records.)

Fort Morgan was noted for its ornate sandstone entryway. This September 1864 photograph shows that the entrance received only superficial damage during the siege, although a 15-inch

shell struck perilously close. (National Archives and Records.)

At dawn on August 23, 1864, when the Confederate garrison asked for terms of surrender, the Citadel, the garrison's barracks, was a burned out shell. After the surrender, Union occupation forces lived in tents outside the walls of the fort. In this view looking east from Bastion 2, the tents of the Union camp fill the landscape. (National Archives and Records.)

In 1999, the view from the same location shows how the area has changed since the Battle of Mobile Bay. (Fort Morgan Museum.)

Four

THE ERA OF BIG GUNS

By the end of the Civil War, military planners realized that the nation's massive coastal forts had outlived their usefulness. Even the impressive array of iron cannon possessed little value against long range rifled artillery. Despite an attempt to modernize the entire system in 1867, Fort Morgan was abandoned and fell into disrepair. But the old fort's service did not end. During the presidency of Grover Cleveland, new designs for fortification originated with a committee headed by Secretary of War William Endicott. By the 1890s, work began on new concrete construction at Fort Morgan. Between 1895 and 1904, five reinforced concrete batteries rose from the sands. These incorporated the latest technological developments in fire control, electricity, and communications.

As the fort's mission changed and expanded, the army constructed new buildings. Most of these were built of wood. At the peak of operations between 1910 and 1918, more than 100 structures dotted the Mobile Point landscape. But by the early 1920s, advances in weaponry rendered Fort Morgan's concrete batteries obsolete. To cut expenses, the Army ordered the deactivation of Fort Morgan by January of 1924. Eighteen years later, another garrison arrived on the post to serve in another war.

—Michael Bailey

Fort Morgan's Coast Artillery companies, the 99th, 75th, and the 170th, assemble for dress parade on the post drill field around 1908. Both the 99th and 170th were organized at Fort Morgan, the 99th on August 8, 1901, and the 170th on January 9, 1908. The 75th Coast Artillery was organized in 1901 at Fort Preble, ME, and transferred to Fort Morgan in July 1907. The

company served there until December 1912, when it left for Hawaii. The 99th served at Fort Morgan for 12 years, before moving to the Philippines in December 1913. The 170th remained at Fort Morgan until the company was reorganized during World War I. (National Archives and Reports.)

Civil War–era ordnance at Fort Morgan waits to be scrapped during the early years of the 20th century. The four guns in the background are 100-pounder Parrott rifles that made up part of the fort's armament during the 1870s. In the foreground, minus its breech, is a Confederate copy of a U.S. 30-pounder Parrott rifle. The gun is mounted on an iron British pattern casemate carriage. There is no documentation on how or when this gun or carriage came to be at the fort. Both gun and carriage survived the scrapping and are displayed at the fort. (Fort Morgan Museum.)

During the Civil War, brick forts did not fare well in contests with Union naval forces. After the war the Army sought ways to improve its seacoast defenses. In the 1870s, 12 200-pounder Parrott rifles were mounted on the barrette level of Fort Morgan. An ambitious plan calling for the construction of detached batteries around the fort was abandoned when Congress refused to fund the additional changes. (Fort Morgan Museum.)

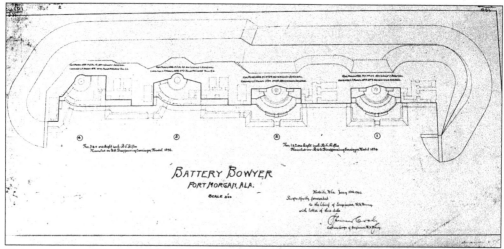

Construction on Fort Morgan's first concrete battery, Battery Bowyer, began in 1895. Although its four 8-inch, breech-loading rifles were manned as an emergency measure during the Spanish-American War, the emplacement was not officially turned over to the Coast Artillery Corps until September 23, 1898. The battery was named for Col. John Bowyer. During the War of 1812 he supervised the construction of the first fort on Mobile Point—Fort Bowyer. (National Archives and Records.)

The 8-inch, breech-loading rifle was the first gun successfully operated on a "disappearing carriage." With a 135-pound charge it could hurl a 300-pound shell almost 8 miles. When bigger guns capable of throwing much heavier shells were adapted to disappearing carriages, 8-inch guns fell out of favor with the Coast Artillery Corps. (Fort Morgan.)

The battery was operational at the beginning of the Spanish-American War in April 1898. Battery I of the 1st U.S. Artillery manned the guns but had no opportunity to fire in anger during the war. Experience proved Battery Bowyer's effectiveness, as part of Fort Morgan's defenses was limited. A relatively light armament of 8-inch guns, the lack of an advanced fire control system, and severe leakage problems in the powder magazines plagued the battery throughout its service. In November 1917, the battery was officially terminated. (National Archives and Records.)

Sgt. Wesley Bailey and his wife, Ruth, pose on one of Battery Bowyer's dismounted 8-inch rifles. Wesley and Ruth met at one of the post dances held while he served at Fort Morgan. (Bailey Collection-Fort Morgan.)

During World War I, Battery Bowyer's four 8-inch guns were removed for conversion to railroad artillery for use in Europe. The guns, loaded on railroad cars, await shipment from the post in 1917. One of these guns, on its railroad mount, can be seen today in Tampa, FL. (Fort Morgan Museum.)

The only surviving gun from Battery Bowyer is shown here on its railroad mount in Tampa, FL. This gun, production #32, was mounted in Emplacement 3 of the battery. (Fort Morgan Museum.)

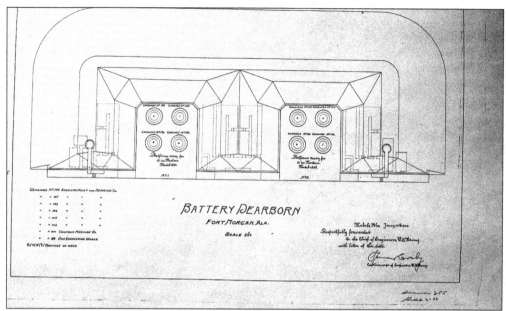

The construction of a mortar battery for Fort Morgan began in 1899. The battery, completed in 1900, was named for Maj. Gen. Henry Dearborn. Born in 1751, Dearborn served with distinction during the Revolutionary War. In 1776 both he and Daniel Morgan were captured during an ill-fated campaign to seize Quebec. From 1801 to 1809 Dearborn was secretary of war in President Thomas Jefferson's cabinet. During the War of 1812 he was the Army's senior major general. He led U.S. forces on the Great Lakes frontier with little distinction until he was relieved of command in July 1813. (Fort Morgan Museum.)

Battery Dearborn's eight 12-inch mortars, each weighing 13 tons, were emplaced in two four-gun pits. The concrete-and-earth placement provided almost total protection from hostile fire while the mortars' high arching fire could pierce the thinly armored decks of attacking warships. (Fort Morgan Museum.)

The breech-loading, 12-inch mortar was a tremendous technological improvement over Civil War–era mortars. These weapons had a maximum range of 7 miles and a minimum range of 1.25 miles. The battery's field of fire was divided into eight zones. Different weights of projectiles and powder charges were used for each zone. Projectiles for the mortars weighed from 824 to 1,046 pounds. When a vessel entered a target zone, all eight mortars fired simultaneously, raining shells down on the intruder's vulnerable deck. (Fort Morgan Museum.)

The rear of Battery Dearborn is shown here lined with the tents of soldiers during the May 1908 Coast Defense Exercises. These drills were the only time the guns on the post were fired at towed targets. The large building in the distance is the post hospital. The partially completed legs of a new metal water tower for the base can be seen to the left of the hospital. The old wooden water tower is to the left of the new metal structure. (Fort Morgan Museum.)

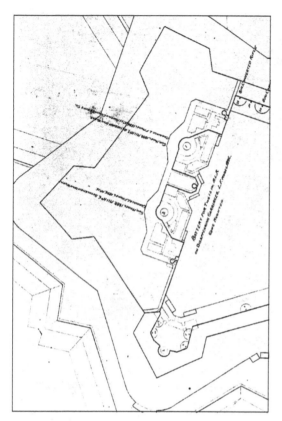

Constructed between 1898 and 1900, Battery Duportail followed a common practice of the Endicott System—the incorporation of new concrete batteries into existing fortifications. At Fort Morgan the battery was constructed across the parade ground, utilizing the old brick fort for additional protection. The battery was named for Maj. Gen. Louis Duportail, a French officer who served with the Continental Army from 1777 to 1783. He was appointed chief of engineers for the Continental Army in November 1777. Captured when Charleston, SC, fell to the British in 1780, he was exchanged and returned to serve on Washington's staff during the Yorktown campaign. (National Archives and Records.)

One of Battery Duportail's two 12-inch, breech-loading rifles on a "disappearing carriage" is pictured here. These powerful guns measured 36 feet, weighed 52 tons, and fired a 1,046-pound projectile over 8 miles. Upon firing, the "disappearing carriage" brought the gun down to its loading position behind the battery wall. This concealed the gun and provided protection for its crew from incoming artillery fire. (Fort Morgan Museum.)

Battery Duportail was the most powerful of Fort Morgan's concrete batteries. Its 12-inch rifles could strike at targets many miles out to sea. Advances in weapons technology during the late 1800s increased the complexity of seacoast artillery. Sixty highly trained soldiers served the battery's two guns. Battery Duportail was the main component of Fort Morgan's defensive network until it was decommissioned in 1923. (National Archives and Records.)

Coast Artillerymen of Fort Morgan's garrison pose for the camera on one of Battery Duportail's massive 12-inch rifles. These powerful weapons were a favorite subject for photographers during the early years of the 20th century. Below the breech of the gun is a sand-filled drip-box to catch grease, which continually leaked from the piece. (Fort Morgan Museum.)

Fort Morgan's Coast Artillery companies assumed war footing for intensive training twice a year. This view of the parade ground, taken from bastion #2 of old Fort Morgan, shows the camp of the 75th Coast Artillery during the Joint Army and Militia Coast Defense Exercise of May 1908. At the left of the photograph can be seen powder cases containing charges for use in Battery Duportail's 12-inch rifled guns. (Fort Morgan Museum.)

Pictured is a direct hit from one of Battery Duportail's 12-inch rifles on a towed target during a firing exercise in May 1908. A 12-inch rifle using a 268-pound charge of nitrocellulose powder could fire a 1,046-pound projectile 8.5 miles. Tugboats chartered by the Army towed large floating targets several miles out in the Gulf along a predetermined course. These firing exercises trained Fort Morgan's Coast Artillerymen to engage enemy navies. (Fort Morgan Museum.)

During the Battle of Mobile Bay, Capt. William Hughes' Company A, 1st Alabama Artillery Battalion, manned the three smoothbore guns in Fort Morgan's Counterscarp Battery. During the 1870s renovation project, Army Engineers razed this battery and began construction of an emplacement for two 15-inch smoothbore guns. Lack of funding forced the abandonment of the project before much had been accomplished. (National Archives and Records.)

A two-gun emplacement was built on the site of the old Counterscarp Battery during the Spanish-American War. This battery, designed to prevent light enemy warships from operating in the ship channel near the fort, was named in honor of Capt. Evan Thomas. Brevetted twice for gallantry during the Civil War, Thomas and most of his command were killed in action with the Modoc Indians at Lava Beds, CA, on April 26, 1873. (Fort Morgan Museum.)

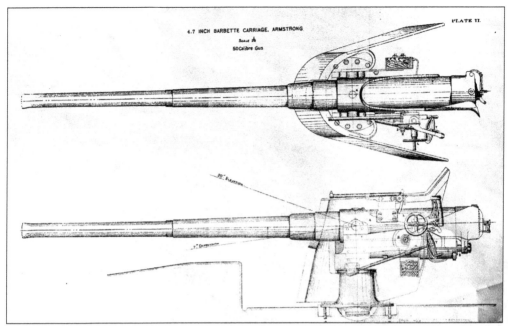

The lack of quick firing artillery produced in this country forced the U.S. Army to use the British-made 4.7 Armstrong Rapid-Fire Gun during the Spanish-American War. This weapon fired a 45-pound projectile 11,000 yards. After the war, as additional rapid-fire weapons became available, the Army gradually phased out these British weapons. Battery Thomas' guns were removed and the battery was discontinued by 1917. (Fort Morgan Museum.)

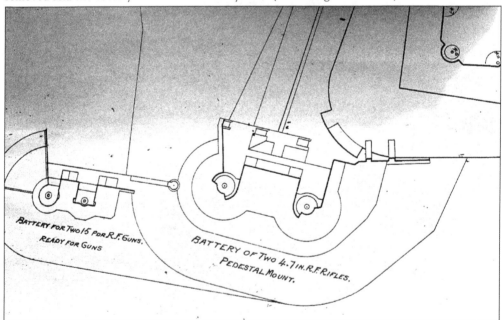

Battery Schenck, completed as an emplacement for two 3-inch rapid fire guns, was expanded in 1904 to mount a third gun. The battery was named in honor of First Lt. William T. Schenck, 25th U.S. Infantry, who was killed in action by insurgents on Luzon, Philippine Islands, on January 29, 1900. (National Archives and Records.)

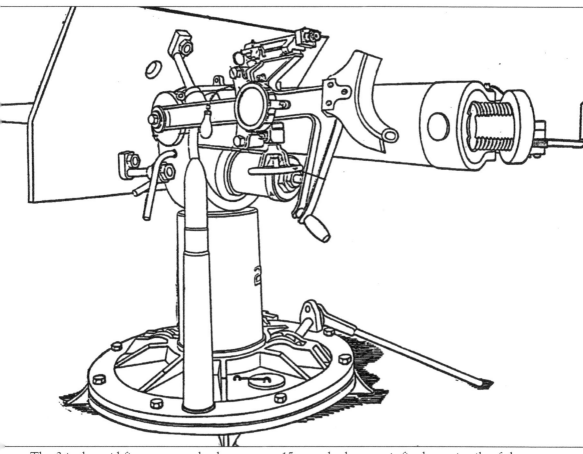

The 3-inch rapid fire gun was also known as a 15-pounder because it fired a projectile of that weight. The 3-inch rapid fire gun at Fort Morgan defended the minefield. Any vessel attempting to remove or neutralize the mines in the ship channel would be smothered with fire from the three 3-inch guns in Battery Schenck. Each gun required a six-man crew and a seven-man ammunition detail in combat.

Batteries Schenck and Thomas guarded the minefield in the ship channel. Their light caliber quick-firing guns protected the mines. This photograph shows two of Schenck's three 15-pounder rapid fire guns. Barely visible atop the large mound is one of Battery Thomas' 4.7 guns. In the distance is the Mobile Point Lighthouse and the lighthouse keeper's house. (Fort Morgan Museum.)

A power plant located in one of the old fort casemates near Battery Duportail supplied electricity to Batteries Thomas and Schenck. These two General Electric generators freed the batteries from dependence on the post generating plant, which was located at the other end of the base and was extremely vulnerable to enemy fire. (National Archives and Records.)

In 1915 the Coast Artillery Corps (CAC) built an experimental battery at Fort Morgan called Battery Test. The position held a single 10-inch disappearing gun manned by target dummies. In 1916 two battleships, the USS *New York* and the USS *Arkansas*, fired on the battery for two days to determine the position's survivability in combat. Drifting sand has now almost completely filled the gun emplacement at Battery Test. Engineers had worried that this would happen before the test firing in 1916. They solved the problem by covering all the sand surfaces of the battery with burlap and then applying a thin wash of concrete to the burlap. Fragments of the concrete wash with burlap imprinted in them can still be found at the battery. (Fort Morgan Museum.)

Officers inspect damage at Battery Test following the shelling of 1916. The battery came through the experiment with remarkably little damage considering that the two battleships involved were among the newest and best-equipped warships in the U.S. Navy. (National Archives and Records.)

So that it could be tested under live fire conditions, Battery Test was built almost a mile from the Fort Morgan complex. Unfortunately, this now leaves it more vulnerable to vandals than the other batteries on the historic site. This photo also illustrates how much sand has drifted into the battery. (Fort Morgan Museum.)

This is Battery Test as it appeared in 1994. The 10-inch gun and its disappearing carriage were removed shortly after the tests in 1916. However, the lever arm, which raised the gun from the reloading to the firing position, was left behind. It can be seen in the center of the photograph. (Fort Morgan Museum.)

As Fort Morgan's coast defense mission expanded at the beginning of the 20th century, the Army constructed many buildings to accommodate the increasing number of troops in the garrison. Over 100 structures had been built on the military reservation by 1910. These included housing for officers and enlisted men, a hospital, a post exchange, a power and ice plant, and a

gymnasium, along with other support buildings. This 1904 view taken from the post water tower looking westward toward old Fort Morgan shows the continuous expansion. The two buildings in the foreground are the Administration Building and the commanding officer's quarters. The post exchange is under construction. (Fort Morgan Museum.)

All supplies for Fort Morgan had to be transported by ship. Contract shipping service out of Mobile proved to be unreliable and expensive. The Army solved this serious problem by assigning its own supply vessels to the fort. Coast Artillerymen are shown here aboard one of Fort Morgan's vessels, the Army quartermaster steamer *S.B. Holabird*, while docked at Mobile. (Fort Morgan Museum.)

The Army directed that barracks in the southern states be "two stories high and have attics with air space enough to keep the second-floor rooms as cool as possible. All barracks and quarters should not only have the windows screened, but the porches as well." This barrack, one of two built at Fort Morgan in 1902, shows that the Army instructions were closely followed. (National Archives and Records.)

Few recreational opportunities for families existed. The extreme isolation of the post made it a constant struggle to keep up the morale of the soldiers and their families. The Army attempted to alleviate some of the hardships by forming social clubs, organizing team sports, and establishing a post library and a school for children. This view depicts a beach outing for military families in 1917. (Bouche Collection-Fort Morgan.)

The garrison enjoyed fishing. During 1914 a group of soldiers of the 39th Coast Artillery displays their catch for the camera and two attentive puppies. (Fort Morgan Museum.)

Organized sports played an important part of garrison life at Fort Morgan. Sporting groups such as the post baseball team, shown here in 1918, provided recreation and promoted unit pride as the fort's athletic teams competed against each other and teams from other Army posts. (Fort Morgan Museum.)

Most of Fort Morgan's garrison was sent to Brownsville in 1914 to guard the border from incursions by Pancho Villa's Mexican revolutionaries. The fort Morgan Coast Artillery football

team defeated a U.S. Cavalry team at Brownsville, TX. (Fort Morgan Museum.)

Louis Pepin and an enlisted man display their catch following a Gulf fishing trip. Pepin served at Fort Morgan twice during his Army career. In December 1913 he joined the post as a first lieutenant assigned to the 170th Coast Artillery. He was transferred to Jackson Barracks in New Orleans a year later. He returned as a lieutenant colonel in 1919 and served as the post commander until 1920. (Pepin Collection-Fort Morgan.)

This company officer's quarters was the residence of Lt. Col. Pepin during his second tour of duty at Fort Morgan. It was one of four similar houses constructed in 1910. Just as with the barracks, part of the house's porches are screened. (Pepin Collection-Fort Morgan.)

Post dances proved to be a popular way to keep up the morale of the Fort Morgan garrison. Young ladies from Mobile received invitations and were provided transportation to and from the fort on the quartermaster department steamer. Fort Morgan's band poses in the gymnasium for a Fourth of July dance in 1913. (Bouche Collection-Fort Morgan.)

The 6-inch rifle, now mounted at Fort Pickens near Pensacola, sits on a disappearing carriage similar to those installed at Fort Morgan. Fort Pickens is a unit of the Gulf National Seashore.

This depicts a 1909 invitation to a dance at Fort Morgan. Hosting a dance posed some financial risks for the sponsors. In March 1919, a post dance incurred expenses totaling $40.38. Proceeds from ticket sales to the dance were only $45, leaving a slim $4.62 profit to be held for financing future socials. (Fort Morgan Museum.)

Wesley Bailey served at Fort Morgan for much of his military career. He was standing guard duty when the steamer arrived with civilian guests for one of the post dances. He saw Ruth as she disembarked and asked her to save a dance for him, and she did. A short time later they married. The couple lived on the Fort Morgan reservation for several years. (Bailey Collection-Fort Morgan.)

Anthony J. Sanfratello was Fort Morgan's boxing champion. In March 1915 he joined the fort garrison as a member of the 39th Company Coast Artillery. Boxing under the name "Tony Dundee" he won the U.S. Army lightweight title in a bout at New Orleans. He served at the fort until 1920. (Sanfratello Collection-Fort Morgan.)

Felix Pepin and Louis Pepin Jr., sons of the post commander, salute the U.S. flag at a retreat in 1919. There were many children at Fort Morgan. The riprap seawall that lines the bayside of the post is visible in the background. (Pepin Collection-Fort Morgan.)

A visit by Navy aircraft breaks the routine of garrison life at Fort Morgan in 1916. Five Curtis N-9 training floatplanes from the Naval Air Station, Pensacola, FL, line the bay beach in front of the 39th CAC barracks while an attentive crowd of soldiers looks on. A plume of black smoke from the post power plant is visible on the horizon. (Fort Morgan Museum.)

Sgt. Eugene Bouche served at Fort Morgan from 1913 until the base's closure in 1923. His military career began in the cavalry in 1910. Although he transferred to the quartermaster department, he never lost his love for horses and continued to ride in equestrian competitions, winning several awards. (Bouche Collection-Fort Morgan.)

Private McDonald is pictured here with Quartermaster Sgt. Eugene Bouche and a U.S. Army horse named "Rex." In the background is the Fort Morgan Post Hospital. The small building to the right is the post morgue and photographic darkroom. (Boushe Collection-Fort Morgan.)

Soldiers of the 39th CAC assemble for inspection in front of their barracks in 1910, possibly during the May Coast Defense Exercises. The leggings the soldiers are wearing show a surprising lack of uniformity in clothing. Three different types of leggings are visible. (Fort Morgan Museum.)

This company barracks day room boasts a pool table. In 1921 Company Standing Order #1 established hours that off-duty soldiers could shoot pool—11:30 a.m. to 1 p.m. and from 4:30 p.m. to taps weekdays and 8 a.m. until taps on Saturdays, Sundays, and holidays. Two lamps light the room, a double burner mineral oil lamp is over the table, and a single burner lamp hangs between the two iron columns. (Gay Collection-Fort Morgan.)

The Army did not forget holidays at Fort Morgan. Each company prepared special meals and menus for the enlisted men. This 1912 Thanksgiving menu for the 170th illustrates the care and preparation that went, not only into the meal, but also into the menu. These special efforts boosted morale and nurtured a strong unit identity. (Fawcett Collection-Fort Morgan Museum.)

The mess hall for the 170th was completed in February 1909, well before the barracks it was to serve. The front room of the building was a 24-by-53-foot dining area. The 26-by-46-foot kitchen wing included two storage rooms and a small sleeping area for the cooks. (National Archives and Records.)

Two civilian workers pose on their mule-drawn garbage cart in May 1908. When the base closed in January 1924, 5,400 feet of brick roads had been built. No motorized vehicles were assigned to the fort between 1898 and America's entry into World War I in 1917. As late as 1919, officers newly assigned to Fort Morgan were advised, "There are no road connections to and from the post . . . There are no facilities for using an automobile at this post." (National Archives and Records.)

Civilian laborers provided much of the manpower that kept the Fort Morgan military base operating. In 1919 there were 72 civilians employed on the post working as boat pilots, carpenters, painters, plumbers, clerks, cooks, and laborers. (Fort Morgan Museum.)

The quartermaster stable, completed in 1908, contained space for 19 animals and 7,250 cubic feet of storage for forage. The 33-by-76-foot-4-inch building included three box stalls and eight double stalls. The stable was still in fair condition when it burned in the 1960s. (National Archives and Records.)

Pvt. Thomas W. Hollingsworth served at Fort Morgan from July 1914 until his discharge in 1915. He stands in front of the stables, where he spent much of his time while at the fort. At one time there were 20 mules and 2 draft horses on the post. Care of these animals was a major concern. In 1909 the quartermaster department recommended that a blacksmith or farrier be employed because of the difficulty involved with travelling from Mobile. (Hollingsworth Collection-Fort Morgan.)

The 99th poses for a group photograph in front of their barracks at Fort Morgan. Organized in August 1901, the 99th was assigned to Battery Duportail from May 1902 through September 1906. From December 1907 until October 1913, the 99th served Battery Dearborn's 12-inch mortars. The company left Fort Morgan on October 30, 1913, for duty in the Philippine Islands. (Fort Morgan Museum.)

In this May 1908 view of a second-floor sleeping area on one of Fort Morgan's Coast Artillery barracks, mosquito netting can be seen over each bunk. This netting was widely used at Coast Artillery posts, especially those in the South. Full-size wall lockers provided storage for the soldiers' clothing and personal effects. A two burner Army barracks lamp lit the room. Fort Morgan's barracks were not wired for electric lighting until 1910. The portable rifle rack holds several of the recently introduced U.S. magazine rifles, Model 1903. (Fort Morgan Museum.)

Between 1908 and 1910 the Fort Morgan garrison increased from two companies to four. This newly completed barracks, occupied by the 170th CAC, is one of two built to house the additional soldiers. The 170th's responsibility for operating and defending the post's minefield is reflected by the two mines that flank the main entrance of their building. (Fort Morgan Museum.)

By 1913, the Fort Morgan Coast Artillery base was well established, as can be seen in this view of the 75th and 170th Companies' barracks. The barracks of the 75th is the earlier 1903-style structure, while the 170th enjoyed one of the two larger newer barracks. Earlier complaints the Army had about landscaping were addressed. Grass and shrubs replaced bare sand; obsolete ordnance decorated the borders of the sidewalks while an electric street light illuminated the area. In the distance one of the post's searchlight towers, with several artillery targets at its base, is visible. (Fort Morgan Museum.)

Cpl. Thomas R. Chess poses at a small work desk in the company day room in 1912. He arrived at Fort Morgan with the 39th in June 1910 and served out his enlistment; the Army discharged him in December 1913. (Chess Collection-Fort Morgan.)

Tragedy struck the Fort Morgan garrison on October 19, 1913. A train transporting troops of the 39th and 170th to a state fair at Meridian, MS, derailed at Buckatunna, MS. Eighteen enlisted men of the 170th and one of the 39th died and almost 100 soldiers were injured, some severely. (Fort Morgan Museum.)

On May 3, 1914, the 39th and 170th left from Fort Morgan for the Texas border to guard against raids by Panacho Villa's Mexican revolutionaries. The company did not return to Fort Morgan until late February 1915. This photograph shows the enlisted men in camp near Brownsville, TX. (Fort Morgan Museum.)

The Administration Building and the guardhouse anchor the west end of Officers' Row in 1911. The two-story Administration Building was moved from its original location to this spot when Officer's Row was expanded in 1908. The photographer stood on the Quartermaster's Wharf to get this shot. (Fort Morgan Museum.)

This aerial view of Fort Morgan, taken from a U.S. Navy flying boat in September 1920, shows the base at its peak. Six World War I temporary barracks buildings can be seen near the old fort. During the war, Fort Morgan served as both a coast defense post and a training base for heavy artillery troops. The fort's garrison increased from a peacetime level of 400 to more than 1,000 soldiers. Additional housing and support buildings were built to handle the increase in personnel. (National Archives and Records.)

With the United States' declaration of war on Germany in April 1917, Fort Morgan's mission expanded to include training Coast Artillerymen in the service of modern weapons in use in Europe. During 1917 and 1918, a number of anti-aircraft batteries were organized and trained at Fort Morgan to serve .75-mm anti-aircraft guns mounted on the chassis of White trucks. (Fort Morgan Museum.)

The increase in enlisted men at Fort Morgan required more medical staff. During World War I, Captain Nelson, surgeon (center) and Lieutenant Graff headed the medical department. (Fort Morgan Museum.)

Col. George F. Connelly is flanked by his staff in this photograph taken near the end of World War I. Born in Ireland in 1868, he served as a first lieutenant in the 7th Illinois Infantry during the Spanish-American War. After that war he enlisted in the U.S. Army and won rapid promotion. A major at the beginning of World War I, Connelly commanded the Coast Defenses of Mobile, headquarters at Fort Morgan, from September 6, 1917, to August 14, 1919. While serving at Fort Morgan he was promoted to colonel. (Bouche Collection-Fort Morgan.)

Taken in May 1908 from the post water tower, this photograph shows the efforts to recover from the devastating 1906 hurricane. The column of smoke in the background marks the location of construction on a 10-foot-high concrete seawall to protect the base from future hurricanes.

The Administration Building was one of the first buildings constructed when the Army reactivated the post in 1898. Completed in November of that year, the two-story, 32-by-40-foot building cost $2,379. The structure originally stood at the east end of Officers' Row, adjacent to the commanding officer's quarters. To make space for additional officers' housing, the Administration Building was moved to the west end of Officers' Row in 1909. (National Archives and Records.)

The Administration Building looks much today as it did when originally completed in 1898. Following Hurricane Danny in 1998, the Alabama Historical Commission renovated this building. (Fort Morgan Museum.)

Of the two senior staff officer's quarters built on the Fort Morgan Reservation, this is the only one that still stands. Begun in 1901 and completed on March 26, 1902, the house boasted ten rooms, two bathrooms, and six closets. (National Archives and Records.)

In the 1980s, the Alabama Historical Commission restored the house to its original appearance. The porch on the left side, removed during the restoration, had been added sometime between 1907 and 1910, probably to provide additional cooling for the house. (Fort Morgan Museum.)

Hurricanes in 1906 and 1916 dealt Fort Morgan particularly hard blows. The wide covered porches that helped cool the buildings proved to be liabilities during these storms. During a July 1916 hurricane, winds reaching 124 miles per hour seriously damaged many of the houses on Officer's Row. The house on the right, the largest house on the post, is the commanding officer's quarters. (Fort Morgan Museum.)

A ground level view of Officers' Row shows soldiers cleaning up the debris scattered by the July 1916 hurricane. The three houses are identical single-family dwellings for company officers. The post water tower looms above the roof of the center building. (Bouche Collection-Fort Morgan.)

The Post Exchange was completed in December 1904 at a cost of $11,743. This two-story, 3,051-square-foot building sold amenities for the soldiers that the Army did not provide. A 1909 quartermaster department inspection report cited the exchange building for an inadequate amount of lunch counter space. (National Archives and Records.)

The Post Exchange fared better in the July 1916 hurricane than many of the other buildings. It survived World War II, but was salvaged for lumber shortly afterward. (Fort Morgan Museum.)

The hospital steward's quarters was completed in January 1899 at a cost of $1,700. The building does not conform to the quartermaster department's plans. The kitchen wing (visible at the rear of the house) was to be directly behind the house, rather than offset to the side. Apparently the modification was made to take advantage of the bay breezes. (National Archives and Records.)

The steward's quarters has outlived most of it grander neighbors. It now stands alone separated by several hundred yards from any of the site's other historic structures. The building is currently used for staff housing. (Fort Morgan Museum.)

The post hospital, completed in January 1899 at a cost of $7,500, provided full medical care for 22 patients. This 1916 view shows that the porches are screened to help the patients escape the ever-present mosquitoes. The hospital stewart's quarters can be seen to the right of the hospital. (Fort Morgan Museum.)

The July 1916 hurricane badly damaged the hospital and its support buildings. The storm destroyed a long section of porch and blew a large number of slate tiles off the roof. The hospital storehouse left its foundation. In January 1919 fire destroyed the hospital. (Fort Morgan Museum.)

Soldiers sift through the smoldering ruins of the post hospital on January 23, 1919. On January 22, a pan of grease left unattended on a kitchen stove caught fire. The uncontrollable blaze destroyed the building. A loss of water pressure at hydrants and the breakdown of "firefighting apparatus" hampered efforts to save the building. No lives were lost and quick action by the hospital's staff and other soldiers saved most of the hospital material before the fire consumed the building. (Fort Morgan Museum.)

The south side of the 39th Company's quarters, one of two barracks completed in 1910, was badly damaged by the July 1916 hurricane. All that remains of the roof of the second-floor porch are the cast-iron bases for its columns. The small building behind the barracks is the company mess hall and kitchen. (Fort Morgan Museum.)

The original post bakery was destroyed in the September 1906 hurricane. This building, completed in February 1908, is its replacement. Although each barracks had its own kitchen and mess hall, the bakery provided bread and other baked goods for the entire garrison. The 1,435-square-foot building had no heating system, as the bake oven and a small cook-stove provided sufficient heat. A Marshall-Continuous Bake oven with a capacity of 470 pounds was installed in March 1908. (National Archives and Records.)

The Alabama Historical Commission restored the post bakery in 1986. Today the exterior of the building looks much as it did when the fort was an active military base. (Fort Morgan Museum.)

Completed in July 1909 at a cost of $13,242, the Ice, Lighting and Pumping Plant was the workhorse of the Fort Morgan reservation. The plant's coal-fired boilers not only powered the generators that ran the post's electrical system, but also kept the water system operating. The ice plant could produce 2.5 tons of ice per day. When the base was closed in January 1924, much of the equipment was left in the building. With no one to maintain it, it quickly deteriorated. In 1939 the building and most of its equipment were reported to be "unserviceable." (National Archives and Records.)

The two firemen responsible for operating and maintaining the Ice, Lighting and Pumping Plant's boilers were part of the Coast Artillery non-commissioned staff at Fort Morgan. As such, they were assigned housing near their duty station. The firemen's quarters were completed in 1910 for $5,395. Each side of this duplex measured 32 feet and 2 inches by 29 feet and 8 inches. Although the building was reported to be in "fair" condition in 1941, it was scrapped shortly after World War II. (National Archives and Records.)

By 1919 the Ice, Lighting and Pumping Plant required 111 tons of coal each month. To provide dry storage, a coal shed was built adjacent to the plant in 1911. The 32-by-165-foot building had a capacity of 1,174 tons of coal. After the post was abandoned in 1924, this structure deteriorated rapidly. In 1936, a hurricane blew it down. (National Archives and Records.)

The tall smokestack of the Ice, Lighting and Pumping Plant fell in the July 1916 hurricane. When the stack toppled it destroyed one of the bins of the adjacent coal shed and was destroyed. Repairs to the shed cost $735. (Fort Morgan Museum.)

In the early 1930s a company unsuccessfully drilled for oil on the Fort Morgan reservation. The Ice, Lighting and Pumping Plant can be seen to the right of the rig and the fireman's quarters is to its left. (Fort Morgan Museum.)

The remains of the Ice, Lighting and Pumping Plant are now almost lost in the thick semitropical undergrowth on Mobile Point. (Bob England Photo.)

When not required at the batteries, powder for the fort's big guns was stored in a "Peace" Magazine. Built in 1902, this 1,462-square-foot structure was located away from the other buildings of the post due to the risk of an explosion. (National Archives and Records.)

"Peace" Magazine is pictured here as it appeared in 1999. Hurricane Frederick blew the roof and the brickwork above the doorways off the abandoned building in 1979. (Bob England Photo.)

This 1930 aerial view illustrates how quickly the base deteriorated once it was abandoned. Many of the support buildings are gone, and all of the temporary World War I barracks are gone.

Battery Duportail stands abandoned and forlorn in January 1937. The Army removed the breechblocks and plugged the breeches when the base was abandoned in 1924. However, the State of Alabama took the first steps toward breathing new life into the site by creating a historic park here. (McWhorton Collection-Fort Morgan.)

The last of eight 8-inch Converted Rifles brought to Fort Morgan at the beginning of the Spanish-American War are shown here abandoned on the brick terreplain. The Army attempted to increase the range and hitting power of obsolete 10-inch smoothbore weapons by inserting a rifled sleeve into the bore, converting it to an 8-inch rifled gun. At least six of these Fort Morgan guns were given to cities for Civil War memorials early in the 20th century. The gun pictured here was apparently scrapped. (Fort Morgan Museum.)

In the late 1930s, the State of Alabama, with the assistance of the Civilian Conservation Corps, began to develop a military history park at Fort Morgan. The massive 12-inch disappearing rifles of Battery Duportail were the centerpiece of the new attraction. (Fort Morgan Museum.)

Five

WORLD WAR II

After the conclusion of World War I, the guns of Fort Morgan lay silent and rusting. National guardsmen and soldiers with the Coast Artillery Corps drilled and maintained the brick and concrete emplacements. A new generation of servicemen arrived on Mobile Point at the outbreak of World War II. Anti-aircraft weapons were installed. The Coast Artillery supported naval efforts to thwart German submarine attacks on shipping in the Gulf of Mexico. The Army, the Navy, and the Coast Guard protected the mouth of Mobile Bay from the threat of German mines. Two 155-mm artillery pieces, mounted on circular tracks, guarded the ramparts. Patrols from Fort Morgan prowled the beaches to the east on the lookout for German commandos and saboteurs. Despite a constant state of war-readiness and a number of alarms, Fort Morgan's garrison engaged no hostile foe. The advent of aerial bombardment made the concrete batteries vulnerable. The Coast Artillery disbanded in 1947 and the post closed, its mission of defense at an end.

—Michael Bailey

The Fort Morgan reservation appears here when the U.S. Army reoccupied the post in April 1942. Many of the Coast Artillery warehouses near the fort early in the century were demolished during the 1930s. (Fort Morgan Museum.)

The train carrying Battery F of the 50th Coast Artillery and its equipment stops at Hamilton, NC, while en route from Quantico, VA, to Pensacola, FL, in April 1942. Battery F arrived at Fort Morgan later that month. (Rogers Collection-Fort Morgan.)

The men of Battery F found these four British-made, 9.2-inch howitzers rusting away in a field when they arrived at Fort Morgan. These World War I heavy artillery pieces were transferred to Fort Morgan in July 1920 in an effort to upgrade the fort's ordnance. After the post was closed, they were turned over to the state for use in the historic site being developed. All four guns were scrapped in 1942. (Rogers Collection-Fort Morgan.)

Most of the movable Army equipment was taken from Fort Morgan in 1923 before the base was closed. This small-gauge locomotive and several flat cars were left behind. When the base was reactivated in 1942 the locomotive was an inoperative rust hulk. It was taken away during a scrap metal drive.

In early 1942 the Coast Artillery brought five model 1918 155-mm artillery pieces to Fort Morgan. Two of these guns were emplaced on top of the fort while the other three were positioned on the post grounds. When the guns were not in use, canvas coverings were kept on the breeches and muzzles to protect them from the harsh environment of the Gulf coast. (Fort Morgan Museum.)

Shortly after their arrival at Fort Morgan, six members of Battery F, 50th Coast Artillery, proudly display their unit guidon behind one of the barracks buildings. The wide range of uniforms worn in the Coast Artillery is illustrated in this photograph. One soldier wears a tropical pith helmet.

Battery Duportail's two 12-inch guns remained in place in 1942 but their days were numbered. The war in Europe proved that the era of the open-topped concrete gun batteries had long passed. Shortly after this photograph was taken, both guns were scrapped. (Fort Morgan Museum.)

Following the scrapping of the two 12-inch guns in Battery Duportail, two 155-mm artillery pieces were installed on top of Fort Morgan on Panama mounts. These simple concrete installations provided an economical way for these heavy guns to track moving targets. (Fort Morgan Museum.)

One of the two 155-mm guns on top of Fort Morgan has just fired and smoke hangs over the dry moat. A parapet of sandbags surround the guns. Panama mounts offered some protection to the gunners in the event of enemy fire.

Troops of Battery F of the 50th Coast Artillery await a full field inspection in front of their shelter tents. The large building dominating the center of this view is the old 170th Coast Artillery barracks. The small structure to the right of the barracks is the kitchen and mess hall building. After repairs these buildings were occupied by Battery F. (Rogers Collection-Fort Morgan.)

The USS *Guide*, a coastal minesweeper, was stationed at Fort Morgan throughout World War II as additional support for the coast defenses. Although Mobile Bay was too shallow for German submarines to operate, there was concern that U-boats would mine the approaches to the bay. (Fort Morgan Museum.)

Seaman Hubbard of the USS *Guide* displays part of the minesweepers armament, an M-1917 .30-caliber water-cooled machine gun. Hubbard was later transferred from the *Guide* to the aircraft carrier USS *Shangri La*. According to one sailor, the mattresses lying around the deck were used by the sailors for sun bathing. (Surridege Collection-Fort Morgan.)

The Engineers Wharf at Fort Morgan continued to serve during World War II. The USS *Guide* and a fast patrol boat are tied up alongside. In the foreground can be seen Battery Schenck, its 3-inch guns having been long since removed. (Rogers Collection-Fort Morgan.)

The U.S. military returned the Fort Morgan reservation to the State of Alabama in 1946. At that time, many World War II installations remained on the site. In the background on the left is the harbor command post that controlled ship traffic in and out of Mobile Bay during the war. The frame tower to the right is the fire control station for the fort's 155-mm guns. (Fort Morgan Museum.)

Following World War II, an attempt was made to convert the reservation into an exclusive resort. The old 170th CAC barracks was fitted up as a hotel and 75th Company barracks was converted to use as a restaurant. An airstrip was developed to enable private planes to fly directly to the site. The resort operated for almost ten years before closing. (Fort Morgan Museum.)

This cast-iron tower replaced the brick lighthouse at Mobile Point. The tower, mounting a 4th order lens, was completed in 1872 and continued in operation until the 1960s. In this 1937 photograph, the hot shot furnace is almost completely covered in vines. (Fort Morgan Museum.)

The U.S. Coast Guard cut down the Mobile Point Lighthouse in 1967 because it interfered with the range board of the new automated Mobile Point Light Tower. In 1994 the old cast-iron tower was restored by the Alabama Historical Commission and erected on a new site about 500 yards northeast of its original location. (Bob England photo.)

A 155-mm GPF artillery piece is shown here on exhibit at Fort Morgan State Historic Site in 1999. In the background are Battery Thomas and the current Mobile Point Light Tower. (Bob England Photo.)

FURTHER READING

Much of the literature on coastal fortifications in American is either highly technical or out of print. But the general reader might be interested in a few books on this fascinating subject.

The best general history of fortifications is Raymond Lewis' *Seacoast Fortifications of the United States: An Introductory History* (Smithsonian Institution Press, 1970). The Smithsonian issued paperback reprints and many bookstores and museum shops keep it in stock. A bit more difficult to find may be Willard B. Robinson's excellent *American Forts: Architectural Form and Function* (University of Illinois Press, 1977). To fit Fort Morgan's story into the larger fabric of American national defense history, I recommend *For the Common Defense: A Military History of the United States of America* (Free Press, 1984) by Alan R. Mellett and Peter Maslowski. The book offers a fine introduction to its subject.

Books on the Civil War are too numerous to know where to begin. Jack Friends' brief bibliography adequately covers Admiral Farragut's victory at Mobile Bay. Though there is no comprehensive treatment of the siege of the Mobile Bay forts, the Alabama Department of Archives and History and the Fort Morgan museum possess excellent collections.

Though Raymond Lewis' general history introduces the Endicott fortifications, the best general history of a battery from this period is Walter K. Schroder's *Dutch Island and Fort Greble* (Arcadia Publishing, 1998). Though not about Fort Morgan, the book has excellent illustrations of the technology of coastal defense.

Two organizations specialize in military sites. The Council on America's Military Past publishes a journal, a fine newsletter, and hosts a conference each year. Membership information may be obtained by writing to the following address:

Camp
518 W. Why Me Worry Lane
Phoenix, Arizona 65021

The Coast Defense Study Group publishes an excellent quarterly journal. This organization concerns itself primarily with the Endicott and modern area of coastal defense. Because of the emphasis on engineering and technology, the articles in the journal tend to be highly specialized. CDSG hosts a tour and study conference at a major coastal defense site each year and is composed of a wide variety of men and women with many interests.

Coast Defense Study Group
Elliot L. Deutsch
1560 Somerville Road
Bel Air, Maryland A 21015-6027

Anyone with an interest in Fort Morgan and Mobile Point's history should consider joining the Defenders of Fort Morgan. The organization initiates a number of fine projects each year in cooperation with the fort's staff.

Robert C. Neibling
Treasurer
Defenders of Ft. Morgan
P. O. Box 3914 / Gulf Shores, Alabama 36547

About the Authors

Blanton Blankenship received his M.A. in history from Louisiana State University. He has served as manager of Fort Morgan State Historic Site for 10 years.

Michael Bailey is a graduate of Auburn University in Montgomery. A long-time employee of Fort Morgan State Historic Site, Bailey serves as curator of the museum.

Bob England graduated from Samford University, and received his M.A. in history from the University of Montevallo and his Ph.D. from the University of Alabama. He is president of the Defenders of Fort Morgan and a professor of history at Northwest-Shoals Community College.

Jack Friend is a graduate of the Virginia Military Institute. He served as an officer during the Korean War, is a leading authority on the Battle of Mobile Bay, and is a member of the Alabama Historical Commission.

Postscript

The Alabama Historical Commission administers Fort Morgan. Through a wide variety of preservation and conservation activities, life at Mobile Point from the War of 1812 through World War II is presented and interpreted. Summer programs feature living history demonstrations and guided tours of the property.

The importance of Fort Morgan to our history lies in the tangible remains of successful efforts to thwart the invasion of the country from the sea by a foreign power. When lessons learned in the Civil War pointed toward new directions in coastal defense, the response of the Endicott Board produced an advanced system of weaponry and fortifications that stood guard until the advent of aerial bombardment. The old brick fort, completed in the 1830s, and the modern reinforced concrete batteries provide eloquent testimony to 19th-century American defense needs.

FORT MORGAN TERMS

FORT MORGAN
ALABAMA

BANQUETTE: The raised masonry step behind the parapet, sufficiently high to enable the defenders, when standing upon it, to fire over the crest of the parapet with ease.

BASTION: A projection from the fort wall, usually at the corners, which allows flanking fire along the walls.

CASEMATE: Vaulted bombproof chamber with embrasures for artillery. Casemates provide overhead protection for gun crews and allows tiers of cannon be stacked. They also provide firing positions for small arms and may serve as quarters, storage areas, kitchens, and other functions.

CITADEL: A small stronghold built within the walls of the fort. It serves as a barrack and is intended as a refuge for the garrison in which to prolong the defense of the fort after the main walls have fallen to the enemy.

COUNTERSCARP: The outer masonry wall of the ditch built to make the ditch as deep as possible.

CURTAIN: The portion of the scarp wall that lies between two bastions and joins their two flanks together.

CUNETTE: A narrow drainage ditch in the middle of the dry ditch.

DITCH: The low, dry area located between the scarp and the counterscarp walls that inhibits the passage of the enemy to the scarp wall.

EMBRASURE: An opening in the scarp wall which allows a cannon to fire through.

GLACIS: The gentle slope beyond the counterscarp wall, cleared of all obstructions, which an attacking enemy must cross to reach the fort.

PARADE: The open area in the center of the fort, usually used for drilling troops.

PARAPET: The low masonry wall along the top of the fort which protects the cannons and the banquette.

SCARP or SCARP WALL: The perimeter wall of the fort.

TERRA PLEIN: The level masonry area immediately behind the banquette and parapet.

CPSIA information can be obtained
at www.ICGtesting.com
Printed in the USA
BVHW091309150721
612042BV00004B/523